I0606052

THAT'S STRANGE!

THE MYSTERY OF D. B. COOPER

Tom Jackson

Lerner Publications ◆ Minneapolis

Lerner Publications Company
An Imprint of Lerner Publishing Group, Inc.
241 First Avenue North
Minneapolis, MN 55401 USA

For reading levels and more information, look up this title at www.lernerbooks.com.

Main body text set in ITC Franklin Gothic.
Typeface provided by International Typeface Corporation.

Library of Congress Cataloging-in-Publication Data

Names: Jackson, Tom, 1972–author.
Title: The mystery of D.B. Cooper / Tom Jackson.
Description: Minneapolis : Lerner Publications, [2025] | Series: That's strange! (UpDog books) | Includes bibliographical references and index. | Audience: Ages 8–11 | Audience: Grades 4–6| Summary: "In 1971 a man hijacked a plane and demanded parachutes and money. Then he jumped out of the plane and was never seen again. Readers will discover the strange, unexplained story of D. B. Cooper"—Provided by publisher.
Identifiers: LCCN 2024010708 (print) | LCCN 2024010709 (ebook) | ISBN 9798765648186 (library binding) | ISBN 9798765662526 (paperback) | ISBN 9798765659076 (epub)
Subjects: LCSH: Cooper, D. B.—Juvenile literature. | Hijacking of aircraft—United States—Case studies—Juvenile literature.
Classification: LCC HE9803.Z7 H543 2025 (print) | LCC HE9803.Z7 (ebook) | DDC 364.15/52092—dc23/eng/20240313

LC record available at https://lccn.loc.gov/2024010708
LC ebook record available at https://lccn.loc.gov/2024010709

Manufactured in the United States of America

1 – CG – 12/15/24

Table of Contents

This Is a Hijack!

In 1971, Dan Cooper took over a plane.

He told the crew he had a bomb. They better do what he said!

The plane arrived in Washington. Cooper was given $200,000 and some parachutes.

He ordered the plane back into the air.

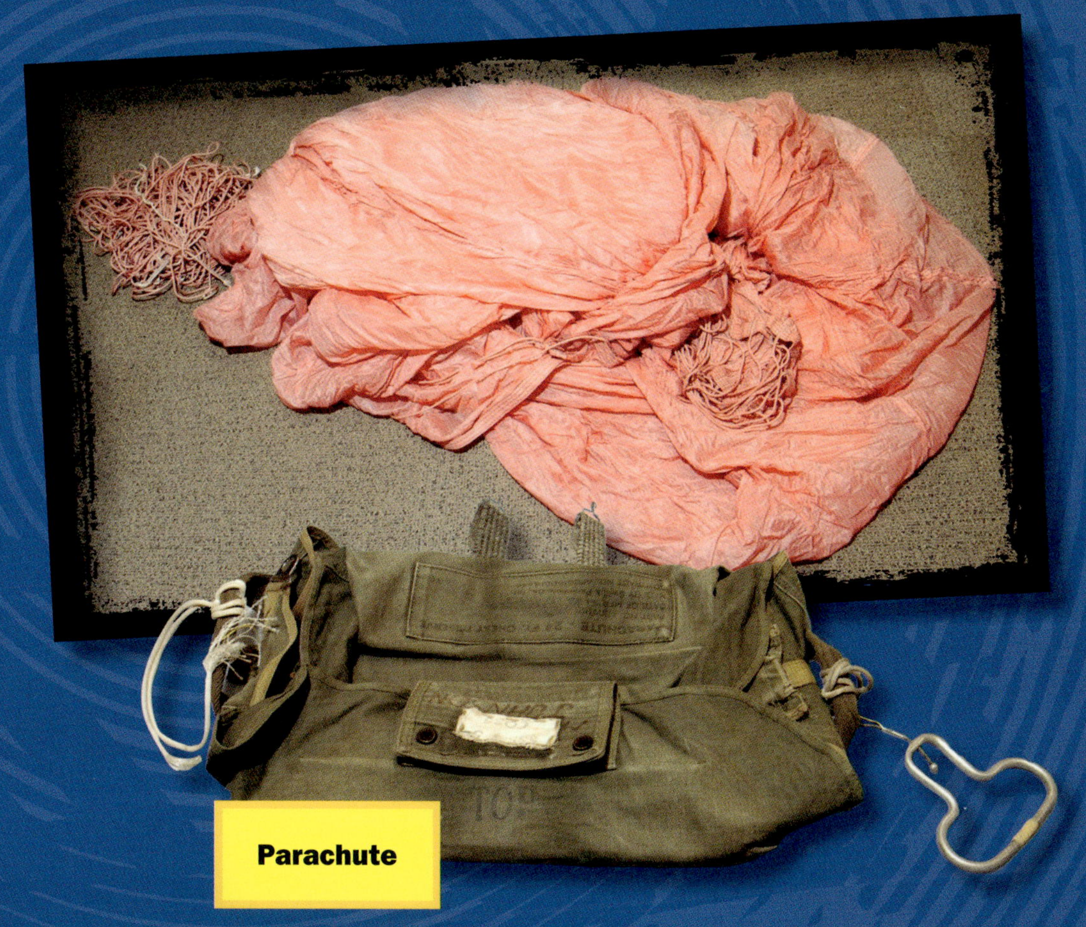

Parachute

The plane flew. Cooper opened the plane's door. He jumped out with the money.

He was never seen again. Who was he?

UP NEXT!

THE FACTS!

A Daring Plan

The flight started as normal.

Then Cooper showed the crew what was in his briefcase. They could see wires and what looked like dynamite.

Cooper's ticket

The plane landed.
Cooper got his money.

He let the passengers go.
He then asked for more fuel.

The plane took off again.

Cockpit door

The crew stayed in the cockpit. No one saw what happened next.

The plane landed in Nevada. The back door was already open.

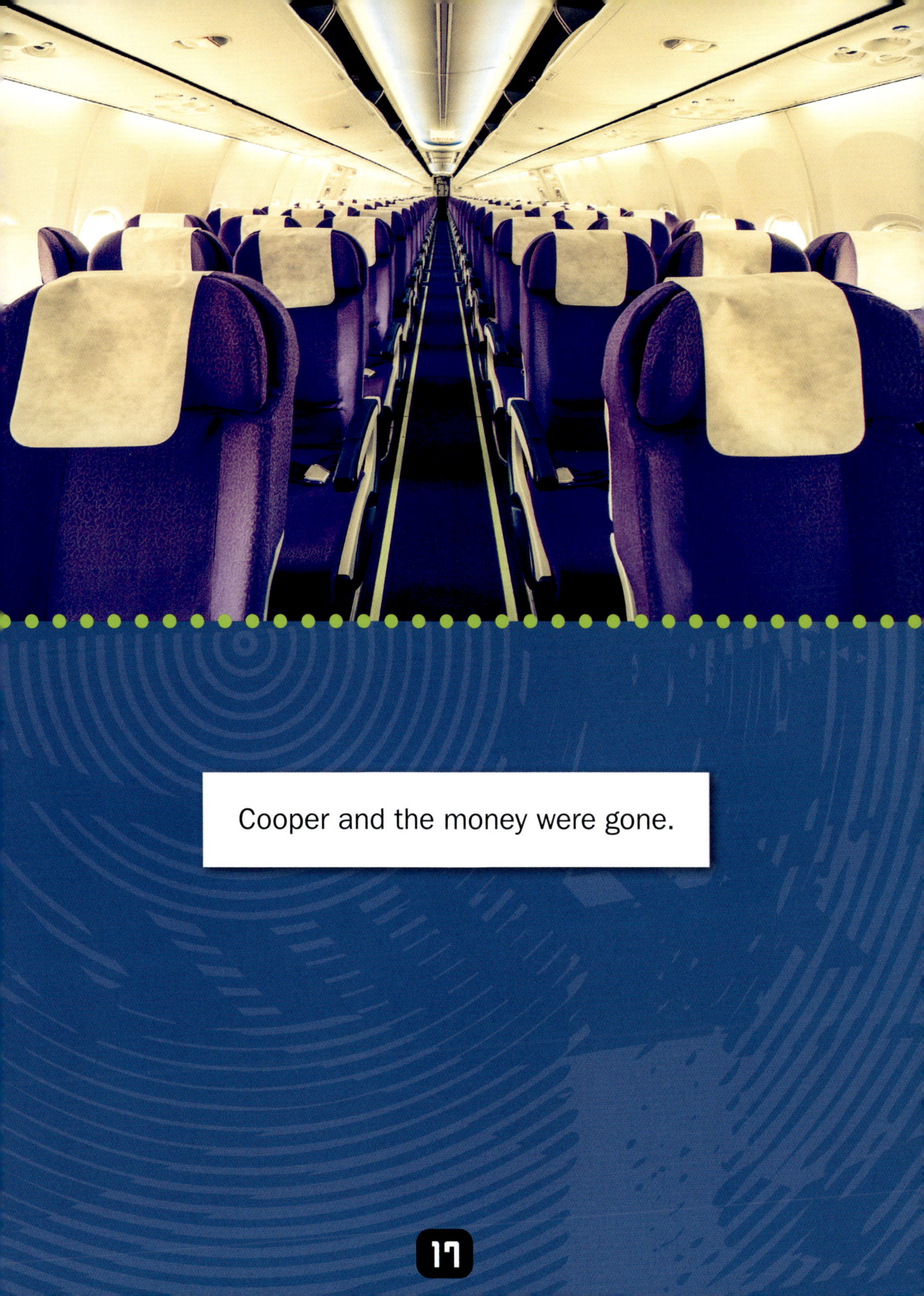

Cooper and the money were gone.

List Break!

What do we know about D. B. Cooper's hijack?

- Cooper skydived from the plane.

- He left behind only his black tie.

- Many years later some of his money was found in a forest.

D. B. Cooper's special skills:
• He could skydive.
• He knew a lot about planes.
Was Cooper an aircraft worker?
UP NEXT!
FINDING CLUES.

Gathering Clues

Cooper jumped into a forest.

It was dark and cold.
The police searched.
They found nothing.

In 1980, a boy found a packet of $20 bills in the area.

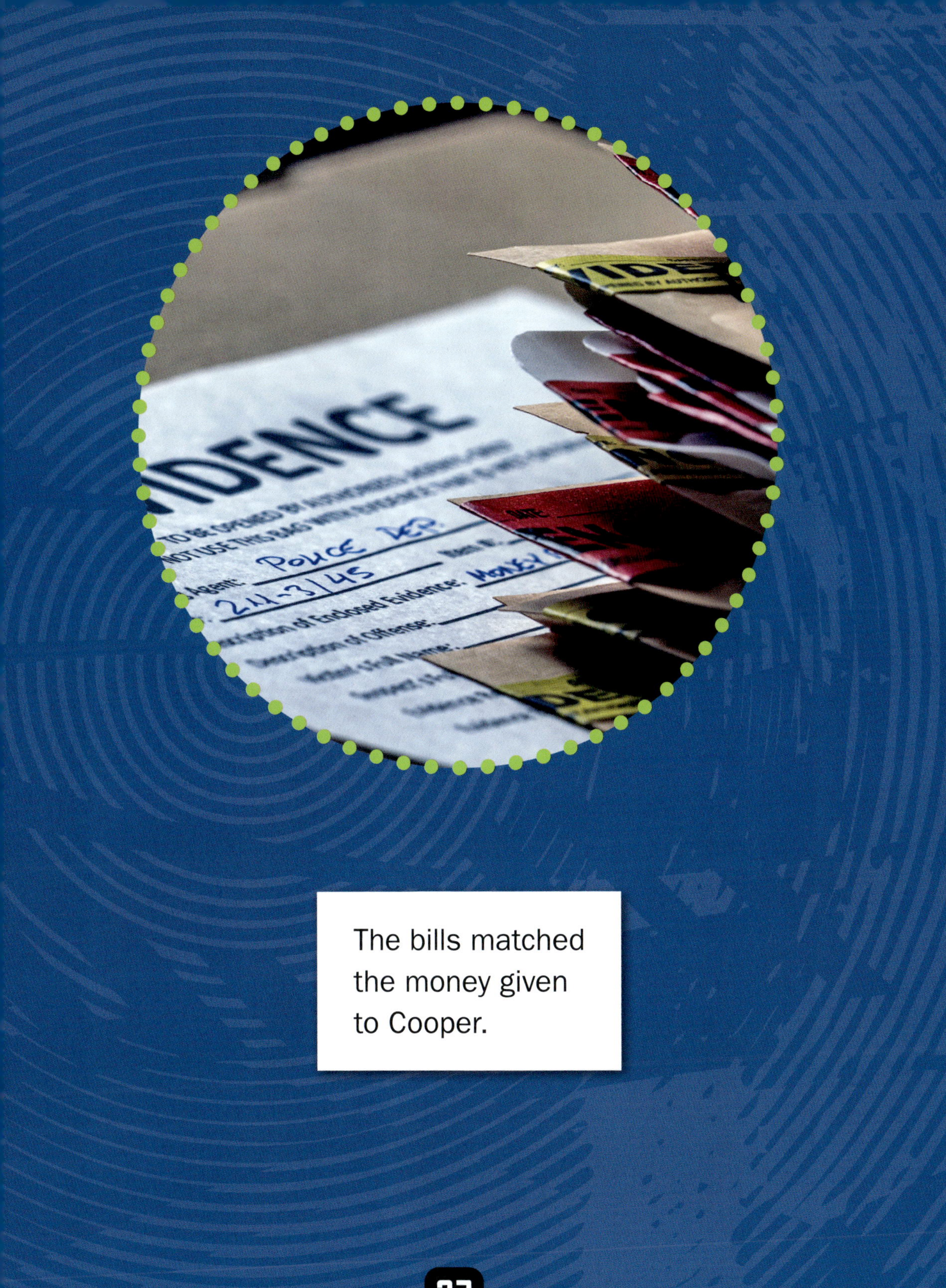

The bills matched the money given to Cooper.

Cooper left his tie on the plane.

The police found DNA on it. This could identify Cooper one day.

UP NEXT!

THE SEARCH FOR COOPER.

Who Was D. B. Cooper?

Reporters got the name wrong.

The hijacker became known as D. B. Cooper.

Cooper knew a lot about planes.

Was he a soldier?

Or maybe he built aircraft?

Will this mystery ever be solved?

Glossary

briefcase: a small suitcase for carrying papers

cockpit: the place at the front of an airplane where the pilot sits

DNA: a chemical that is unique to each person

dynamite: an explosive made into long sticks

hijack: when a criminal takes over an airplane

parachute: a large cloth that slows a falling person so they land safely

Check It Out!

Academic Kids: D. B. Cooper
https://academickids.com/encyclopedia/index.php/D._B._Cooper

Bell, Samantha. *12 Suspenseful Mysteries*. Mankato, MN: 12 Story Library, 2020.

Kiddle: Federal Bureau of Investigation Facts for Kids
https://kids.kiddle.co/Federal_Bureau_of_Investigation

Ringstad, Arnold. *D. B. Cooper.* Mendota Heights, MN: Apex, 2023.

Social Studies for Kids: The Enduring Mystery of D. B. Cooper
https://socialstudiesforkids.com/articles/ushistory/dbcooper.htm

Streissguth, Thomas. *Investigating the D. B. Cooper Hijacking*. New York: AV2 by Weigl, 2020.

Index

Photo Acknowledgments

Image credits: 3d_man/Shutterstock, pp. 3, 19 (top); lends 16/Shutterstock, pp. 3, 18 (top); Aero Icarus/flickr.com, p. 4; sketches/FBI.gov, pp. 5, 9; Dana Rothstein/Dreamstime.com, p. 6; parachute/FBI.gov p. 7 (top); parachute bag/FBI.gov, p. 7 (bottom); Salienko Evgenii/Shutterstock, p. 8; Rawpixel.com/Shutterstock, p. 10; Elnur/Shutterstock, p. 11 (top); plane ticket/FBI.gov, p. 11 (bottom); Carlos Yudica/Shutterstock, p. 12; Office2005/Dreamstime.com, p. 13; EvrenKalinbacak/Shutterstock, p. 14; Xavier Marchant/Dreamstime.com, p. 15 (top); Aliaksandr Bukatsich/Shutterstock, p. 15 (bottom); Reno–Tahoe_International_Airport_16_L_photo_D_Ramey_Logan/Wiki Commons, p. 16; tratong/Shutterstock, p. 17; black tie/FBI.gov, pp. 18 (bottom), 24; Pressmaster./Shutterstock, p. 19 (bottom); SnappPhoto99/Shutterstock, p. 20; The Adaptive/Shutterstock, p. 21; money/FBI.gov, p. 22; felipe caparros/Shutterstock, p. 23; gpixa/Shutterstock, p. 25 (top); create jobs 51/Shutterstock, p. 25 (bottom); Pixel-Shot/Shutterstock, p. 26; eveleen/Shutterstock, p. 27; Peshkova/Shutterstock, p. 28 (top); Getmilitaryphotos/Shutterstock, p. 28 (bottom); santi lumubol/Shutterstock, p. 29. Design elements: sokolovski/Shutterstock, pp. 1–32.

Cover: sokolovski/Shutterstock; sketches/FBI.gov; ArtMari/Shutterstock.